Humor and
Moroccan
Culture

Humor and Moroccan Culture

By

Matthew Helmke

A look into the hidden aspects of Moroccan culture that are necessary for understanding local humor.

For more information about this book or to contact the author please write:

Derby & Wehttam · 263, rue Toufah · Hay Zaza · Fes · Morocco

matthew@derbyandwehttam.com

http://derbyandwehttam.com

Please see the "Final Notes and Thoughts" section at the end of the book for more information about this licensing decision.

First edition, published 2007 by Matthew Helmke.

ISBN: 978-0-6151-4284-5

Printed and bound in the United States of America by Lulu, Inc. http://www.Lulu.com

A Moroccan edition is being prepared and will be published by Derby & Wehttam.

http://derbyandwehttam.com

Dedication

This book is dedicated ...

...to my amazing wife, Heather, for her patience and willingness to let me drag her all over the world on yet another adventure.

...to my wonderful children, Saralyn, Sedona, and Philip, whom I love dearly and am more proud of than words can possibly express.

...and to my grandfather, Philip Derby, who always believed in me and who always encouraged and supported my endeavors, even in those times when he thought I was wrong. Thank you for always letting me be me.

Acknowledgments

I would like to thank all my friends and colleagues who helped me edit, fact-check and prepare this book for publication. I sincerely hope I don't forget anyone. Thank you Ouazzani Chahdi Mouhcine for helping me find hundreds of great jokes in darija and for reading and correcting my Arabic transcriptions. Thank you Steve Jones, Mark Renfroe, and Doug Clark for reading my draft manuscript and making incredibly useful comments during the editing process.

I wish I could give credit to the people I interviewed during the research for this book, but nearly all of them wished to remain anonymous. So, I would like to thank all of my friends, who have names like Driss, Mohamed, Rabiaa, and Sanae, without whose openness and assistance this book could not have been written.

I benefited greatly from my time studying Arabic in Morocco at a school called DMG (arabophon.com) and I recommend it highly, especially if you want to learn the Moroccan dialect.

You might be interested to know that this book was created and formatted using free software called Open Office, available at openoffice.org, on a computer running a free operating system called Ubuntu Linux, available at www.ubuntu.com. The book was written and published with the kind assistance of my small business in Morocco, Derby & Wehttam, derbyandwehttam.com.

Table of Contents

Preface

This book will explore and discuss the hidden aspects of Moroccan culture, things that people who grow up in Morocco seem to know inherently. I started on this journey because of a joke. I was living in Casablanca at the time and had been studying Arabic[1]. My friend Mohamed told me a story and started laughing. He reached

---

1 The Moroccan variety called "darija." This is an oral dialect that is generally not written and therefore difficult to transcribe as there are no standard spellings for words. The spellings I will be using are my own and may actually vary from passage to passage...this is not by design, but it should serve to illustrate the more fluid nature of darija. Pronunciations and grammar can change regionally and even from family to family. I will explore this more fully as the book continues.

his hand out to shake mine in a gesture that has now become quite familiar—I like to call it the "we both enjoyed that joke" handshake of congratulation and friendship. As with most handshakes, it is followed by putting your hand on your heart. Unlike other handshakes, it is usually followed by all the parties discussing the joke you just heard and why it was funny. This is to make certain everyone understood it and can be included in the fun. I found the experience enjoyable, even though I had no clue what the joke was about. I was missing something and I didn't know what it was.

I decided to do two things. First, I asked Mohamed to explain the joke to me, line by line. After I learned all the vocabulary and figured out what all the sentences meant, I still didn't think the joke was funny. Mohamed explained it to me, but I didn't understand his explanation. I continued by asking him to explain how things would have normally occurred in that situation and suddenly something clicked. Here was an aspect of Moroccan culture that I had been missing completely. Immediately the joke made sense and I appreciated the humor of it.

The second thing I decided to do was birthed out of

that moment. I decided to ask people, everywhere I could, to tell me jokes. Then I would struggle through each one, trying to understand it, trying to figure out what made each joke funny in its original context. This has led me on a fun, and often difficult and overwhelming, journey of cultural and linguistic study.

Once I had acquired a repertoire of 30 or 40 jokes in Moroccan darija an expatriate friend asked me if I would consider writing them down for him to study. I hadn't thought of that earlier. Most of this still-growing collection was made for my personal benefit and stemming from my personality—I tell jokes all the time in my native language and I love to use them to help make new friends wherever I go. Jokes lighten the atmosphere and mood and help lower defenses. This makes train rides, café visits, and queues to pay the phone bill much more enjoyable.

I wasn't sure how a collection of jokes in Moroccan darija by a foreigner would be received and was pretty skeptical of the idea, so I shelved it for several years. Occasionally, one of my friends among the expatriate community in Morocco would ask me to tell them one of the jokes they heard me laughing over with our mutual

Moroccan friends. I would oblige and translate the joke into English for them. Invariably, the non-Moroccan would not laugh. They wouldn't laugh even when I told it in Moroccan Arabic and they knew every word. From those moments I had an epiphany—you have to understand the cultural tidbit behind any joke for it to be funny. That brings us to the book you hold in your hands.

Each chapter of this book begins with a short story in Moroccan Arabic. These stories were collected from friends, in cafés, in offices, on trains and buses, and in taxis, and even on the street. I have tried to transcribe them as accurately as possible. I am not responsible for the content of the stories, but any errors you may find in transcription, or my sometimes loose translation, are fully mine.

All of the discussion of culture which follows in each chapter is completely mine. My thoughts and insights are based on various interactions I have had with people all over Morocco.

Much of what I state in these pages may come across as authoritative. Please interpret this as a result of my writing style and not my most heartfelt belief. My greatest goal in writing this book is to help the reader begin to ask the right questions when encountering cultural differences and attempting to understand them. Remember, the existence of a correlation between two things does not prove or even imply causation. I make note of many correlations and have hypothesized as to probable causes for what I have witnessed. My hypotheses may be wrong. In any case, I hope that noting the correlations and describing them as best I can may help others to investigate more fully.

All my research for this book has been correlational and anecdotal in nature and never directive nor experimental. I will leave that work for others more qualified than I. In addition, I know that I sometimes oversimplify when mentioning or describing the various influences that bear on decisions and actions in this culture. Human beings are complex and the things that influence us are many. There may be motives and forces in action beyond those that I describe. Please keep that in mind. Look for those things, record them, learn from them, and share them with others.

Finally, I realize that no culture is monolithic and

that the things I describe will not apply to all Moroccans all of the time. In fact, the lion's share of my experience is in Fez, so in some parts of the country my theories might be completely wrong and utterly inapplicable. This has not been intentional, and I have consciously tried to avoid errors, but it's possible errors have crept in.

Being from Fez

قال ليك, هاذا واحد الراجل كان كيمشي في المدينة مع ولده. تلقاو مع صديق الاب و تكلمو شوية. في هذه الواقت سأل الولد منين هو الراجل. قال لي هو من مراكش. بعد شي شوية مشا فحاله. و قال ليه, "ماتسول منين هو." جاوب, "علاش؟ هاد شي عدي؟" قال ليه, "علاحاقاش إلى ماشي من فاس يهشمو و إلى من فاس غادي يقول ليك كلشي."

There was a man walking through town with his son. They met one of the father's friends and stopped to talk a bit. The boy asked the man where he was from and he replied that he was from Marrakech. After a short while they all went their separate ways. The man said to his son, "Don't ask people where they are from." The boy replied, "Why? That's a normal question." The father answered, "If they aren't from Fez they will be ashamed and if they are from Fez they'll tell you all about it."

Fez is an amazing city—just ask anyone who is from there. I happen to live in Fez and I think it is a wonderful place for a large number of reasons. As a foreigner I can appreciate Fez's history, its contributions to Moroccan culture, and its amazing food—which deserves its reputation as some of the best Morocco has to offer. A walking trip through the old city, the medina, is like taking a trip back in time. You will see people living today in much the same way as their ancestors did a thousand years ago, except that today the traders are using their donkeys to deliver Coca-Cola and butane gas cylinders to the neighborhood shops instead of goat skin canteens and freshly cut wood.

In the Fez medina, people buy and sell traditional handicrafts such as fine leather, carved or inlaid wood, and ornately etched or engraved metal. Visitors and tourists explore streets and see homes and buildings that had running water and a sewage system while Europe had yet to emerge from the Dark Ages. One of the more interesting places in Fez for a scholar/researcher is the Qarawiyyin library which is said to be one of the oldest continually used libraries in the world. It has works dating back a thousand years or more and is a library that is still used by students today.

Fez is the home of one of the oldest universities in the world...there seems to be a rivalry between the Qarawiyyin university in Fez and Al Azhar in Cairo as to which is older. Each claim the title and in some sense it appears to be true for each of them. One (I forget which) is said to have been founded earlier, but ceased operating for a short time. I'm told the other started just a few years later, but has never taken a break from teaching. Whether these are facts or rumors, I'll leave the disagreement for others to solve. Both universities are old and well-respected.

Fez is considered the spiritual and intellectual capital of Morocco. Its residents consider themselves, perhaps rightly so, to be some of the best educated and most sophisticated people in the country.

Fassis[1] are proud of the fact that no invaders were ever able to enter the city walls and conquer the city. Fez is a fiercely independent city that has historically held very

1 The name for a person from Fez is "fassi" much like someone from Marrakesh would be called "marrakeshi" and so on.

strong opinions and great sway politically, religiously, and culturally. In addition to being the unquestioned spiritual capital of Morocco, it was also the first political capital and the starting point for the independence movement, which ended the French Protectorate era.

These are all important facts, and the reader must realize that they will color everything that I write throughout this text. I learned Arabic in Fez. I have gained what understanding I have of Moroccan culture based primarily on my years spent here in Fez among my Fassi friends. I have chosen this joke as the first to tell because I am certain if someone reads this book through the eyes of their experiences or friends in Agadir or Tangier, they will have a different perspective or understanding than I.

It's interesting to note that many Moroccans from around the country seem to share the opinions of Fez that I have acquired; that Fez is filled with people who act and believe themselves to be more sophisticated than the average Moroccan, that the history and culture of this city is an old and proud one, and that the city's influence can be felt throughout the country's history. If you were to ask him, a local might tell you a hundred reasons why Fez is an important city historically, culturally, artistically and intellectually. In the next breath he would say that he is not being arrogant, just accurate. Maybe he is right. In any case, this is information that is vital to understanding relationships among people in Morocco.

This trend goes farther than just Fez. Many of the major cities in Morocco have their own special reputation. Casablanca is known as the economic and manufacturing capital of Morocco, Rabat is the French-influenced political capital, Marrakesh is the capital of southern and urban Berber culture, and on it goes. You also have cultural and linguistic differences between people who live in small towns and people who live in big cities, between rural and urban cultures. There is a tension between traditional Berber and traditional Arab ways of life[1]...and

---

1 This is a tension that can be observed by watching people, but one that will generally be denied by Moroccans. The prevailing belief is that there are only Moroccans, that the Berber/Arab dichotomy is unimportant. Amusingly, people who say this will also tell you whether their family is of Arab or Berber descent and often which tribe and geographic region they come from. I think the unity is real in some ways and was necessary in the

another tension as each of way of life is being forced to accept, or at least adapt to, Western ways of thinking and doing things.

A person coming to Morocco for the first time often asks an innocent question, "What is Morocco like?" The answer isn't simple or easy. It depends on which aspect of Morocco you are discussing; a specific family's structure, the socio-economic status of the person you are considering, the physical location, or setting of the location you are interested in. There are many variables and each one can have a major impact on the answer to the question.

So, now you see why the Moroccan father in the joke told his son not to ask where people are from. And, like anyone from Fez, I have told you more than you wanted to hear.

---

struggle for independence from the French Protectorate.

I'm not sure that is Arabic

هادي واحد مدرسة و فيها أستاد جديد. بغى يعرف سميات ديال التلاميذ ديالوه. و بدى يسولهم، "شكون أنت، شكون أنتي." جاوبوه، "أنا محسن. أنا نزهة." و قال ليه واحد التلميذ، "أنا أسم." شاف فيه الأستاذ و فكر، "شنو هدا؟ ماشي سميى هادي." و طلب منه إعاود ثاني مرة وعاو ثاني قال ليه "أنا أسم." فكر المعلم و قال، "لا. أنت ماشي أسم، أنت <u>قاسم</u>." جاوب الولد، "هاذا لي ألت لك" علاحقاش هو من مدينة فاس حيت فاسى ماكيقولوش "ق". قال الأستاذ بلي خصو يتعلم يقول مزيان هاد الحرف مهيم. ظرب المعلم الولد حتى قالها صحيحة. سول الأستاذ ولد أخر و طلب منو سميتو. ولد خاف بزاف و قال ليه، "أنا قحمد."

There was a new teacher in the school and he wanted to know all the kids' names. He asked and they began to respond, "I'm Mouhcine. I'm Nazha." One boy responded, "I'm Asim." The teacher looked at him and thought, "That isn't a real name. What's going on here?" He asked again and again the boy responded, "I'm Asim." The *teacher thought a little more and told the boy, "No, your name isn't 'Asim,' your name is '<u>Qasim</u>.'" "That's what I said," repeated the boy, who was from the region of Fez where they don't pronounce the letter "Q." The teacher told him that this is an important letter. To teach him to pronounce his name correctly, he hit the boy until he said it right. The teacher then looked at the frightened boy next to him who replied, "I'm Qahmid."*

Where ever you go in Morocco you will discover that no matter how good your Arabic is, it is not the same as the people you are with. Dialects and accents can change from one neighborhood to another, and certainly from one city or region to another. Moroccan darija also differs significantly from Modern Standard Arabic, also known as Fous-ha.

The boy in the story is from a specific part of the old city of Fez. In that area people tend not to pronounce the letter "qoph" or perhaps substitute a "hamza"[1] in it's place.

---

1 A glottal stop that sounds like an unvoiced "a," like the sound you make in English when you say "uh-oh."

The teacher is from another part of Morocco, it could be a different city or even just a newer part of Fez. He doesn't speak with the same accent and had a hard time understanding the boy. This is actually very common, even for Moroccans traveling within their own country. Just as an Englishman might have trouble understanding an American from the Cajun parts of Louisiana, a Moroccan from the rural Souss plain in the south might have difficulty communicating with another from urban Casablanca.

To get this joke you need one more vital bit of information. The name Qasim is common enough for people to know it well. In the region around of Fez many would pronounce it just as the boy pronounced it, without the first letter. The name Hamid is also common and would start with the same sound as the boy's accent-modified pronunciation of Qasim.

The second boy also grew up in the same part of Fez and realized part of what was going on. He had not traveled outside of the area and suddenly became afraid that every word he had ever heard starting with a hamza now needed a qoph. That would have included his name.

In an attempt to avoid a beating, the boy unnecessarily adds the additional letter to his name, just like his friend was forced to do.

I have found when traveling, that a person is not considered an Arabic speaker unless he has learned the local dialect. No matter how well you can read and write, no matter whether you are able to speak beautiful, flowing, classical Arabic, unless you can sit in a café and have a casual conversation, you will not be considered an Arabic speaker. Some allowance is made for travelers, say someone from Rabat visiting Tangier. If you can make yourself understood, that will be sufficient, even if your pronunciation is very different.

It is for this reason I consider it useful to travel and listen to different Moroccan accents when possible. I attempt to adapt my speech when I am in a new area. I've learned some interesting tidbits, but I know much more remains before me.

In Fez and surrounding areas, an active verb is indicated by a "k" sound at the beginning, preceding the standard conjugation. In Rabat, this changes to a "t" sound. In other places, no sound is attached at all.

For the letter used in the joke, ق – qoph, some places will pronounce it deep in the throat like in Modern Standard Arabic. Other areas will change it to a "g" or a "â"[1] or even a "k" sound.

This is what makes transcribing darija so difficult. It makes a joke told in one area and transcribed using phonetic symbols quite difficult to comprehend for someone who has learned darija in a different region.

Also of note, in Modern Standard Arabic you have to be very careful when pronouncing a word. The careless changing of one short vowel can render a completely different meaning.

Moroccan darija bypasses this complication by omitting short vowels much of the time. This causes the language to sound very staccato and even harsh to the untrained ear.

Moroccans can understand the Arabic from places like the Middle East, but people from those regions usually find Moroccan darija incomprehensible. One good reason for this is that much of the media produced for the

---

1 ع, or "ayen."

Arab world comes from either Lebanon or Egypt. Most Arabic speakers are familiar with those dialects. Morocco is the only place I know of where people watch television shows and movies produced by Moroccans in the Moroccan dialect. This adds to the general perception among Moroccans that their native tongue is inadequate, or something to be embarrassed about. I disagree. I believe darija is a rich and amazing language that is just beginning to discover it's potential.

There are almost no books written in Moroccan Arabic. Newspapers, most television and radio broadcasts, and intellectual interaction occur in either Modern Standard Arabic or French. These are languages that are completely foreign to Morocco and inaccessible to the half of Morocco that is functionally illiterate. It is only in the last few years that Moroccans have begun to create art, music, and literature using their native darija, but there is still very little. In addition, there is also a movement among the Berbers of Morocco to begin teaching and using their native language, Amazigh, as well. This is creating some interesting controversy.

Communication in Morocco varies widely in style,

accent, and even language. Whether you are traveling from town to town, region to region, or simply from home to home, you will discover a wide variety in the manners, customs, and languages used within Morocco. I continually find myself talking to Moroccans and discovering that each of us are using words from three or four different languages within the same sentence. I'm amused that neither of us consider this odd.

Visitors from the Arab Middle East tend to say, "I don't think these Moroccans are speaking Arabic." I agree. They speak Moroccan. You can call it "darija," you can call it "Moroccan Arabic," you can even call it a "panache of languages." I'm not sure you should call it, "Arabic."

Always exceed expectations

هادا واحد الولد في المدرسة كسول بزاف. ديما مادايرش تمارين ديالو. قال ليه المعلم جيب باك. فاش جابه قال ليه المعلم ولدك مكلخ. جاوبو الراجل ولدي ذكي بزاف. جا المعلم قال للولد سير قلب علي في القاعة خمسة. مشا الولد وعي يقلب. و جا رد على المعلم و قال ليه ماسبتكش. جا باه ظرب الواد و قال ليه إلي ماصبتيش في القاعة خمسة قلب عليه في القاعة ستة.

There was a boy attending school who was very dumb and he never did his homework. The teacher told him, "Bring your father here." The father arrived and said his son is very smart. The teacher told him to watch and sent the boy on an errand saying, "Look for me in room five." The son returned and said, "You weren't there." The father hit his son and told him, "If the teacher tells you to go to number five, you go to number six!"

All parents want their children to do well in school.

They long for their kids to learn and have as many options for the future as possible. It is a real hope for most parents that their kids will have a better life than they enjoy. Moroccan parents are no different. The father in this story wants his son to study, learn, and excel in school. This will increase the boy's chances of getting a good job and having a comfortable life in the future. He wants it so much that he tells the boy, in a colloquial fashion, that no matter what the teacher asks of him, the boy needs to exceed those requests and expectations.

This is a beautiful part of Moroccan culture... unfortunately it is a belief that isn't held by all and is sometimes derided as being old fashioned or silly. There is an extreme societal pressure to succeed and a widespread societal shame attached to failure. Even so, some people say that you should only do what you are required to do in order to get by, that you should take life easy and not worry about the consequences. The attitude displayed by the father is one that is more traditional and it is still held by many in the society, especially those that end up in places of power, money, status or authority.

It seems that both the son, and the original creator of

the joke, have had significant contact with people who do not share these cultural mores. The joke is that the father is trying to teach his son the right lesson, but without fully understanding what the teacher has been saying. "If the teacher tells you to go to number five you go to number six," makes no sense when discussing looking for a person whose location is already known, and yet its meaning is clear enough. It's not adequate to simply fulfill your requirements, you should go above and beyond them.

Why didn't the father understand? That really is the crux of the joke. Over the past 50 years or so, since Morocco regained its independence, there have been amazing and drastic changes in this society. Some of the changes began under the French protectorate era and have simply continued. Many of these changes are the result of new technology, easier forms of travel and communication, and the move from a predominantly rural, agrarian society to a predominantly urban, manufacturing and industrial society. Some of these are factors that societies are struggling with, or have worked through, everywhere in the world.

The father is a poor man, probably from a rural

setting, who holds to traditional values. His beliefs and culture are in direct conflict with some of the changes he is witnessing in the society at large. It would not be an exaggeration to call him a symbol of a much larger group within Moroccan society.

This group has faithfully supported three kings since independence[1], Mohamed V, Hassan II, and now Mohamed VI. The elders of this group have watched their land go from having few roads, almost none of them paved, to having modern highways. Train access is available now in all major cities and many of the smaller ones. Other recent changes involve airplanes, telephones, electricity, running water, radio and television. The list continues with the introduction and rapid spread of mobile phones and high speed internet access. The bulk of these modern conveniences are considered a blessing by members of this social group, even though they bring with them societal changes that are difficult and uncomfortable.

The sad part of living in the midst of rapid change is that some people, while witnessing and experiencing the

---

1 In the case of Mohamed V, well before independence, during the struggle to achieve it, and afterward until his early death.

change, can also be left out of it. This sub-group within Moroccan society is overwhelmingly favorable toward the government, education, and "modernization," whatever that specifically means to them. Yet, many of them have not personally benefited the way their children, grandchildren, and future generations have and will. Amazingly, most don't seem to care so much about that.

In general, members of this generation have an outlook on life that is longer in scope than what people growing up in already fully industrialized societies tend to have. This group tends to think in terms of generations, not years. They are content to see changes occur if they believe it will truly benefit their heirs, even if they themselves are not privileged to share in the benefits. What a beautiful perspective!

The author of this joke is pointing out this very fact. It is as if he is saying, "Poor man. You want your son to excel, but you don't know what you want him to excel at." Therein lies the tension. The father sees all that has happened around him and he is convinced that it is for good. He believes that his son will benefit if the son will work and study, but he has no idea what the son is being taught and no way to comprehend what the boy is being told to do. For the father the phrase "Go to number five" could mean anything, but because he has an innate trust in the leaders, the educators, and the government, he tells the boy to go beyond, and "go to number six."

Some might say this joke is a mean swipe being taken at an undeserving segment of society. I tend to see it, however, as someone from the younger segment that has benefited, trying to make sense of his most recent ancestors' generation and sacrifices. The story is funny because it has an unexpected twist at the end, but it is sad as well. Many of those who have worked hard to enable Morocco to achieve the wonders it has achieved in such a short time, have been unable to share in the benefits of their labor.

Don't give me advice

واحد نهار جحا مشى لعند صحبه و طلب منه بزاف د الفلوس. هو قال له، "علاش بغيتيهم هادوك الفلوس أ جحا؟" جاوبو، "أنا غادي نشري فيل." سول صحبو، "فيل؟ أش كتفكر جحا؟ ماعندكش بلاسة كبيرة باش يعش فها الفيل. ماعندكش الفلوس باش تشري ليه المكلة. أش كتضن يا صحبي؟" جوب جحا، "أنا طلبت منك فلوس، ماشي نصحة."

One day Juha went to his friend's house and asked him for a large amount of money. His friend asked him, "What are you going to do with that much money, Juha?" Juha answered, "I'm going to buy an elephant." "An elephant?" his friend responded, "What are you thinking, Juha? You don't have a place big enough for an elephant to live in. You don't have enough money to buy food for an elephant? What are you thinking, my friend?" Juha answered, "I asked you for money, not advice."

Juha is an interesting character in North African, and Middle Eastern folklore. He is similar to the Mullah Nasser ed-din in Turkey. He's part jester and part wise man. He can say what everyone is thinking, but would never say, and he can get away with it. Sometimes stories about him impart wisdom, sometimes they're just amusing observations of human nature. In every case, though, there is some tidbit of insight into the human condition that comes from a Juha story.

In this story, Juha asks his neighbor for money. This is a more common occurrence in Morocco than in many of the places I have been. Life here seems to retain some aspects of ancient tribal culture that are not understood elsewhere. People live at a more communal level. The ideas of individualism and self-reliance are considered a bit odd and extremely selfish. The prevailing perspective is one based on community.

Decisions are usually made with respect to how they will affect the family, not just what might be best for the individual. Nice things that are purchased by one family are generally available to be used by the family's friends and neighbors, if and when there is a need. For example, no one needs to buy all the necessities for a large party. If one family has a large pot, they will lend it freely to a friend that needs it. In return when they need to borrow their friend's serving tray for a special event, it is available. These are basic understandings and expectations.

I remember one instance when a family bought a new radio. Their neighbors were foreigners and couldn't understand why this family had to play their radio so loudly all day long. When they finally asked the family to please turn the radio down a bit the foreigners were greeted with a bemused expression. You see, the family thought that playing the radio loudly was an act of kindness. They knew that not everyone in the building had one, so they were trying to share.

How different that is from the standard in my home country, where we expect to never hear our neighbors unless we are each outside at the same time and intentionally turn to greet one another! We have expressions like, "Good fences make good neighbors," and believe that the best way to get along while living in close proximity is to live so that no one else knows we're here. We also say, "Neither a borrower nor a lender be." Imagine how I was taken aback the first time a Moroccan neighbor came to me and asked if he could borrow something of mine.

What Juha has done is perfectly natural in his home setting, even if he was asking for an extremely large amount of money. If it was within his friend's power to give it to Juha, he would. What's more interesting is that the friend would be likely to give, even to the point of self-deprivation if necessary, to help a friend or family member.

When asking for help, Juha knew there would be strings attached. Whenever someone does something for you, especially if it is done by your request, you are obliged to repay the favor in some way. There is a cultural expectation or reciprocity in friendships and relationships that cannot be eliminated. For this reason, some people will limit the number of close friendships they have. They may even choose to only be friends with people in their extended family or clan. This doesn't mean that every time a person does something for you he is trying to get something from you. It is, however, very easy to be perceived as greedy or ungrateful by not reciprocating hospitality.

It is common for conversations in Arabic to be more direct than they are in English. An English speaker would not likely say to his friend, "What are you thinking?" unless he was truly shocked or offended. There are linguistic and cultural reasons for this. In Arabic, the passive voice is rarely used, especially in casual and informal conversation. Instead, things are said using a more declarative and definite form of expression. In the place of, "Do you think that's wise?" a more common way to question behavior would be to say, "What, are you crazy?" In place of, "Do you like this?" you are more likely to hear, "This is great, isn't it?"

In order to communicate in a different culture and language, you need to learn more than vocabulary and grammar. You may be able to translate the words and even the main ideas of a conversation. Without understanding what is and is not polite, the subtext of a conversation is very easily misunderstood.

Now to the punch line. There are two things going on here worth noting. First of all, it is typical when someone requests something of you to either say "Yes" and give it to them, or "God willing, I will be able to do that for you later." The second response implies you love this person asking so much that you would never refuse a direct request they made of you, even though there is no possible way you could ever fulfill this request[1]. You might say, "I'm so sorry, please excuse me, I would love to help but there is no way I can." This third response is not typical, but is still within the bounds of politeness, because it allows the one making the request to save face, it shows him respect.

The first time I heard this joke I thought Juha's friend was being rude and demeaning to Juha and was reacting to him out of anger. That isn't how my friend, who told me the joke, thought of it at all. What we are witnessing is the casual banter of two close friends having fun one with another. Just as you might say something to your best friend that you would never say to someone else (eg. "Go jump in a lake!" or worse), Juha's friend is trying to get away with not giving Juha the money by making a

---

1 In this case, the answer is understood to be "no" even though it is never said.

joke himself. He expresses his shock at Juha's plan through an inappropriate form of refusal. Then Juha says what no one else could get away with, "I just want your money, not your advice."[1]

---

1 This implies that Juha thinks his friend's money is more important than his friend's thoughts, and even more important than the friend himself. No one except Juha would ever say something like this unless he intended to offend.

Who are you going to trust?

واحد نهار جى عند جحا صحابو و طلب يسلفو حمار. قال جحا،
"حمار ديالي ماكاينش." فهذه الوقت الحمار ديال جحا بدا يغوت
بصوت علاي. و سمعو صاحبو، "قلتني بلي هو ماكيانش." جوب
جحا، "شكون كتيق واش أنا ولا حمار؟"

*One day Juha's friend came to his house and asked to
borrow Juha's donkey. Juha said, "My donkey isn't here."
At that moment the donkey began braying loudly. Juha's
friend heard it and said, "I thought you said the donkey
isn't here." Juha replied, "Who are you going to believe,
me or a donkey?"*

As noted in the previous chapter, the things Juha
says and does are not always right. They do, however, tend
to contain some interesting information about cultural
values. Here we have another instance of borrowing and

lending behavior being twisted slightly. You can guess from our earlier discussion that Juha was supposed to let his neighbor use his donkey. In most instances that would be true. Exceptions to this expectation would be made if Juha had need of the donkey for work, or if the animal was in need of rest because it had been used recently, or because it would be used soon. None of these cases seem to apply.

Juha tells his friend the donkey isn't there. He doesn't embarrass his friend by saying, "You can't use my donkey." That would shame his friend. It would be saying that the donkey was more important to Juha than his friend. Apparently Juha just doesn't want to lend it out. This presents a problem for Juha. How can he refuse his friend's request while allowing the friend to save face? Simple, he tells a lie. This really is the lesser of two evils in a place where lying is far less of a crime than subjecting someone to humiliation.

A friend of mine in Jordan has heard the same joke told with the additional information that Juha's neighbor had previously and repeatedly borrowed the donkey, always returning it in worse condition. In that instance,

Juha could be saving his friend's face by choosing not to confront him about his poor treatment of the donkey and instead covering up the friend's shame with a lie.

Some parts of Moroccan society are well adapted to a more Western style of thinking in this regard and have no trouble discussing what they will do, when and how. For these groups it doesn't matter at all if I ask them a direct question, they will answer truthfully with a "yes" or "no." For others, however, especially those who are more traditional in their upbringing and personal demeanor, a direct question can create a genuine conundrum. If they are able to say "yes" honestly, it is done with great joy and exuberance. If they really can't do what I am asking them, however, they will never tell me "no."

In those cases the, "yes, God willing[1]," is said with enough exuberance for me to believe it is something they genuinely want to participate in or do, but with an attempt to communicate to me via subtext that what I am asking is really impossible, unless God intervenes supernaturally. The difference is quite subtle and the cues can change

---

1 In Arabic, إن شئ الله

from family to family or even person to person.

I have decided not to ask certain of my friends direct questions, if it can be avoided. This way, they are not put in a position where they feel they have to lie to me, either to save their face or mine. For example, instead of asking, "Will you come to my house on Friday?" and always receiving an answer of, "Yes, God willing," and wondering if I will actually see the person Friday or not, I will now ask, "Are you free on Friday? I'm thinking of making a special meal." In this way my friend can answer honestly, "I can come, what time were you thinking?" or, "I'll be traveling to Rabat on Friday so I can't be there." The difference is small but it is an important one, since clear communication is the goal. Instead of saying, "May I come and borrow your ladder tomorrow?" I will ask if the ladder is available for people to borrow, which will sometimes elicit a, "No, I don't like to lend it out," or a, "when would you like to use it?" Admittedly, this is a workaround solution and is not perfectly natural for the society. Even after five years of living in Morocco, I still find it too easy as a foreigner to confuse a, "Yes, I will definitely do that," and a, "Yes, that will happen if God performs a miracle to change the current circumstances, but I love you too much to say anything else." This is how I have adapted.

Back to Juha and his friend. Juha lies to save his friend's honor, while at the same time covering up his own (rather selfish and societally shameful) desire not to lend his donkey. Then the donkey exposes the fraud. What can Juha do? He can't tell a more obvious lie and say a donkey didn't bray. He can't admit to lying without humiliating himself greatly and causing his friend shame.

The friend violates societal norms as only close friends can do. He pushes the issue with Juha. "I thought you said the donkey wasn't here." He's teasing Juha by saying the equivalent of, "Dude, you just lied to me. The donkey's braying right there, we can both hear it!" Juha wins by upping the stakes immensely, "Who are you going to believe, me or a donkey?"

In this society, the three worst names you can call a person are dog, Jew, or donkey (and not necessarily in that order). Use any of the above three names and you are likely to find yourself engaged in an angry and ugly fight.[1]

Morocco is a country where people are legally free to practice their religion and where I have lived as a Christian peacefully alongside a massive Muslim majority (qbout 99%) and a small Jewish population scattered around the country. Stories have been told to me by dozens of different people about how, for over a thousand years, the Jewish people have been welcomed in Morocco and have lived here as an important part of this society. I

---

1 While I can't address this racist attitude as I would like to in this book, I would like to mention the following observation. The way Morocco has dealt with Jews through it's history has been mixed. One beautiful event occurred a few years before independence. During the rise of Nazism in Germany, Hitler sent a message to Mohamed V saying that in return for the expulsion of all Jews from Morocco, he would support and fight for Morocco's right to self-rule. Mohamed V replied that there are no Jews or Muslims in Morocco, no Berbers nor Arabs—there are only Moroccans. On the other hand, at independence in 1956 there were 300,000 Jews in Morocco out of a total population of ten million. Today there are about 5,000 in a land of over thirty million people. Most Jews have emigrated to Israel. Discussing why would require further research so I'll leave that alone for now.

certainly have no desire nor means to argue with the prevailing opinion of the masses, but I cannot deny that every time I have heard someone call someone else a Jew (who is not one) a fight has broken out. Juha doesn't take it quite that far, but in Moroccan society a donkey is only better by a small degree.

To solve his problem Juha forces his friend into an uncomfortable situation. To answer Juha's question, the friend must either say Juha is less than a donkey (at the risk of losing his friendship forever), or say that the donkey is lying and cause himself embarrassment. No wonder the friend's answer isn't recorded.

I won't let you buy that

كان شي راجل مشى لمحل و قال لالمواظف تما، "أفاك، بغيت هذه التلفيزة." جوبو بلي ماكييبيعوش لعروبي. ألراجل مشى فحاله و بدئ يقرى باش يحسن لغته. شرى حوايج جداد كيف عندهم ف المدينة. بعد عام هو يرجع و طلب عود ثاني بغيت التلفيزة. جوبو نفس الشئ، "ماكييبيعوش لعروبي." قال الراجل، "كيفاش عرفتي أنا من العروبية؟ الحواج ديالي مزانين، قريت بزاف و دابا كنتكلم جدا بلهجة مزانة. شنو؟" جاوبو، "هذه ماشي تلفيزة، هذه ماشين الافي."

There was a man from the country who went to a store in the city. He said to the worker there, "Please sell me this television." The man answered him, "We don't sell those to country people." The country dweller left, went home and began to study to improve his language skills. He bought new clothes like the ones people wear in the city. After a year, he returned to the store and asked again, "Sell me that television." The answer was the same, "We *don't sell those to country people." The man asked, "How did you know I'm from the country? My clothes are nice. I studied hard and now I can speak well with a good accent. What's going on?" The worker answered, "That's not a television, it's a washing machine."*

Once I was visiting in Rabat and I took my family for lunch to a well-known international pizza restaurant. We sat down, looked at the menu, everything was familiar to us. We thought about it a while and decided to buy more pizza than we needed, so we could take some back to our hotel to eat for dinner later. That way we wouldn't have to go out in the evening when the kids were tired.

The waiter returned and I ordered the largest pizza on the menu for my family. He told me it was too big for my family and that I can't order it. Amused and a little shocked, I presumed I must have misunderstood. I asked him again to please bring us the largest pizza on the menu. He kindly and patiently told me that pizza is designed to feed 8 people and there were only 4 of us sitting there. That would be too much pizza for us. I tried explaining that we wanted to get extra to take with us afterward to eat later. He looked at me quizzically and walked away.

Moments later the manager of the restaurant appeared and spoke to me in English. I told him we would like to order the extra-large pizza please. He said, in a beautiful British accent, that I can't order that pizza because it is too big for my family, but he would be happy to bring us an appropriately sized pizza with the same toppings. I relented and we ended up eating dinner at the hotel restaurant that night.

Anywhere I go, in any store, no matter what I try to buy, the first question is invariably, "Why do you need that?" or "What are you trying to do?" Everyone wants to make sure I don't buy something I don't need, whether I think I need it or not. I've had the automobile dealer absolutely refuse to perform maintenance early, even after I told him I wasn't worried about the cost, that I was planning to take a long trip, and I didn't want to worry about my oil, filter, tires, or whatever. This trend can be amusing, frustrating or helpful depending on the situation.

I got to thinking one day about how this social norm came about. I noted previously that this is a community based culture, not an individual based culture. Decisions are made using a different standard than I am used to. In the United States, for example, if someone wants to buy an item, and they have the money to pay for it, the shopkeeper gladly makes the exchange. After all it isn't any of his business whether the person needs the item or not, and it can always be returned if there's a problem.

I think there are several reasons for people's reticence to sell you things in this culture. First of all, returns are only allowed if the item is defective, and even that is only true in a small number of stores. In most places, the store clerk will open the item in front of you and show you how to use it. He will even plug it in if necessary to make sure it functions properly before you leave the store. Why? Because once you give him your money the transaction is final. You can't return things in most places, and you can never return an item just because you don't need it, you bought the wrong thing, or the color didn't match when you got it home. The clerk who refuses to sell you an item you don't "need" is trying to protect you from the disappointment you are sure to experience if he lets you leave with an item that is unsuitable for your needs.

That leads me to the second reason. It is an unspoken rule here that the strong should always protect the weak, that the educated will look out for the interests of the ignorant, that those with means will help the poor. The safest assumption a store keeper can make about his clients is that they do not know what he knows about his products and their uses. Therefore, he must protect them from their own ignorance. He must tell them which is the best product that will suit the customer's needs. This is a way to ensure repeat business, especially if the clerk is good at his job.

When I tell this joke, no one is surprised or amused at the clerk's refusal to sell the television set to the man, they generally applaud it. How is the clerk to know whether the man has electricity in his house? What if the man spends a large amount of money to buy the set only to get it home and discover there is no broadcast signal available for him to watch? If the country dweller doesn't know the difference between a television and a front-loading, glass-windowed, clothes washing machine, how can he be expected to understand and answer all these sorts of more detailed questions? No, the sales clerk is a hero because he's taking care of his fellow man, a man who might mean well, but who appears to be ignorant.

The part people laugh about is that someone could find a way to earn enough money to buy a new television (they aren't cheap in Morocco) and somehow not learn how to distinguish one from a washing machine. Here's another example of a class of society that wants to be a part of all the change occurring around it, but has thus far not fully benefited.

What encourages me is that I can't recall anyone laughing at this joke in any way other than simple amusement. It's a funny problem, but I don't see people mocking the country dweller for his ignorance.[1] Instead, people who have told these sorts of jokes to me chuckle at the silliness and proceed to tell me how important it is to take care of people in this situation and that it is our duty to protect one another from making big mistakes.

---

1 Some of my friends who read the manuscript told me they have heard this joke and similar ones told in a way that does mock the ignorance of these people. For the sake of completeness I want to note that my experience is not universal.

Respect is more important than truth

هادا واحد البوليسي كان قبيح بزاف. ديما كان كيطلب من الناس رشوة. واحد نهار ماوقف حتى شي حد. ملي لقى الشمس تمشي فحالها و ماعنده فجبو والو قال البوليسي، "أنا خصني فلوس. غنوقف الاول لي يجي." بعد شوية جى راجل راكب موتور جديد. مول موتور عنده كاسك، خدام مزيان الموتور، البوليسي ماعندوش سبب باش يوقفو ولكن شدو. شاف وراقو و كلشي كان بخير، ماكاينش فاش يطلب من مول موتور. سوله، "واش ماتخافش؟ علاحقاش بواحدك." جوب مول موتور، "أنا ماشي بواحدي. معيا الله و الرسول." قال البوليسي، "ثلاثة؟ فوق هاد الموتور؟ خصك تخلس."

There was a policeman and he was corrupt. He always stopped people and asked them for bribes. One day he worked all day and didn't stop anyone. He realized as the sun was going down that he didn't have anything in his pocket so he said to himself, "I'm going to stop the next person I see." Shortly thereafter, there came a man riding a new moped. The moped appeared to be working fine, the man was wearing his helmet, but the policeman stopped him anyway. The man's papers were all in order and the corrupt policeman couldn't find a reason to ask for a bribe. He said to the man, "Aren't you scared to be riding out here all by yourself?" The man answered, "I'm not by myself, I have God and the Prophet with me." The corrupt policeman responded, "Three of you on that little moped? You'll have to pay a fine."

I have had an internal debate for months whether to include this joke or not. It was told to me in Casablanca years ago and I assumed Morocco had changed, that the joke was an extremely old one and that nothing like this could happen in a country that is so set on modernization and which speaks so consistently about the rule of law. Then I got stopped by a policeman for no reason and he asked me for a bribe.

Before anyone protests, I will own up to deserving a fine or two. I have been stopped while speeding and willingly paid the price I deserved to pay. I have also been stopped while speeding and experienced mercy at the hands of a policeman who gave me a warning and sent me on my way. In addition, I have been stopped at security checkpoints at random. These things are not unusual nor frustrating. In this instance, however, I can honestly say I had done nothing wrong.

I was driving in Rabat. As I passed through an intersection, the traffic light turned yellow. The policeman was a little bit further down the road. When I arrived to where he was, he pulled me over and told me the light was red when I entered the intersection, and that I would have to pay a fine.

My first thought was that I don't want to upset this guy, so let's just see what's going on. He asked me for my papers and we had a nice conversation in Arabic about my life, where I live, what I do for a living, and so on. He then handed me my papers back without filling out a traffic report or ticket.

Next he told me that the fine for my "infraction" was 400 Dirhams (about $45 US Dollars at the time) and he asked me if I wanted to pay the fine. I looked him straight in the eye and with an incredulous expression and asked, "Of course not, why would I *want* to pay a fine?" It was at this moment that I was informed of another way to solve the problem.

The policeman asked me what I was going to give him (to his credit, he never actually used the word "bribe"). I gave him my "dumb" look and said, "What do you mean?" Then we went through the "do you want to pay the fine?" series of questions/responses again. He said again, "What are you going to give me?"

It was a very hot day and I had a brand new, unopened bottle of cold water sitting beside me on the passenger's seat. I picked up the bottle and offered it to him. He responded by saying that was nothing and he could buy his own water, pointing out a store across the street. "What are you going to give me?"

So I did it. I told him this joke. Now, I was cautious. I repeatedly said things like, "I know nothing like this could ever happen in Morocco today," and, "He is nothing like you, I know you're a good man, an honest man, just trying to keep people safe on the road." I made sure to give the policeman lots of eye contact while embellishing the tale as much as I could—it probably took me 5 or 6 minutes to tell it. At the end I began laughing hysterically.

I asked, "Isn't that funny? Three on one "motor[1]!" He asked him to pay! Ha ha ha ha ha..." and stretched out my hand for the policeman to shake.

The policeman looked at me uncomfortably and laughed a little bit. He shook my hand. He then said meekly, "Is the water cold?" I gladly gave him the bottle and he waved me off.

So what happened here? Well, for starters, as I told the story, I continually praised the police officer and his country. The only way he could claim I had done anything insubordinate or inappropriate would require him to claim I had said something specific against him or his country. I hadn't, at least not directly. The police officer wasn't willing to lie about this and cause me shame because that would elicit a very strong, combative response in this culture. I allowed him to save face, and he made sure my honor remained intact as well. In retrospect, I'm not sure this would have worked if a third person had been present.

Another possible reason this worked is that if the

---

1 A moped or vélomoteur, it's like a bicycle with a motor or a small, underpowered motorcycle with pedals you crank to start the motor.

policeman had claimed that it was my intention to say something against him or Morocco, after I had explicitly said the opposite, then he would be admitting that *he* thought there was something wrong with his country. That is what would be required to draw this conclusion since I had been so insistent in saying the opposite. There was no way the policeman would shame himself by admitting that he had even entertained the thought that he might be dishonest or that there might be something wrong with his country.

All of this is true because Moroccan society has traditionally been based on a system of honor and shame. Unlike the West, where the values held most dearly include things like truth and justice, Morocco and other eastern cultures prize honor and respect above all. Honor comes from how you are perceived by others. If you are a good man you will have certain character traits. This will earn for you the respect of the community.

Gaining or losing the respect of others is a primary motive in social interaction; actions are chosen based on how others will perceive the actor, not necessarily on an objective standard of right and wrong. Shame is what one feels when the community perceives a person in a poor light and their status is diminished. The quickest way to initiate a fight is to do something that causes shame. The easiest way to earn someone's favor is to help them gain honor. Your actions and words will communicate what you think of the person, whether you think they are important or not, good or bad, valuable or worthless. I have found that people here tend to become what your words and actions imply you think they are. If you treat people with great respect they act more respectable when they are around you. If you treat (most) people as if they are trustworthy, they strive to be worthy of the trust you place in them.

The question remains, did the policeman understand what I was saying? Did he know I was calling him corrupt and telling him he shouldn't ask people for bribes? Of course he did. However, telling him in this way allowed him to hear the message without any direct assault on his honor. He wasn't happy with me, but there was no cultural basis for him to rise up and defend his honor because his honor was not attacked.

As I drove away the policeman said one last thing to me. We had discussed this book as I was in the early stages of writing it. He called out after me as I drove away, "You're not a writer, you're a preacher!"[1] I'm completely certain he understood the point of my story.

One of the more difficult aspects, for an American adapting to this culture, is learning how to effectively communicate disagreement, disappointment and frustration without causing people unnecessary shame. While there are moments when causing someone to lose face is necessary and even desirable, these are the exceptions, not the rule. In general, I believe that it is a good idea to try to live at peace with all people, as much as it is within your power. Communication in this manner is an art form that has been practiced and improved upon over thousands of years.

It is not necessary in Morocco to refrain from voicing your opinion. On the contrary, telling people what you think is vital for friendships and other relationships to work. The art comes in the method of self-expression.

---

1 "انت ماشي كاتب، انت خاطب" He used the informal title of the man who gives the sermon in the mosque after the Friday prayers.

How do you tell someone you think they are wrong without making them feel as if their honor is at stake? Here are a few ideas I have picked up.

Stories are useful tools, especially if they are humorous in nature. Humor takes the edge off of bad news and a good story will make your point as clearly as if you said what you were thinking directly[1], but because it is someone else who is the direct object of the action your listeners won't feel personally attacked, or at least will feel that their honor is intact.

If you can learn traditional proverbs and maxims in the local language you will endear yourself to your hosts and give yourself a way to say what you are thinking, without putting yourself on the hot seat. Calling up a bit of ancient, sage advice can be invaluable.

This also works in English. If someone is doing things slowly we might say, "The early bird gets the worm," in an attempt to speed him up a bit. If he is going too quickly and doing a sloppy job we could say, "Haste

---

1 The epilogue of this book contains a good example of a Moroccan doing this. You can read it after this chapter or save it for later.

makes waste." What makes people stop and listen isn't so much what we believe, but rather that the listener recognizes the phrase as culturally appropriate and applicable in the current situation.

In the same way, if my Moroccan friend is trying to learn how to play the guitar but keeps forgetting to bring his instrument to his lesson I could say, "He who does not have pen and ink does not intend to study."[1] Appealing to commonly held "wisdom" is a good way to bring insight and perspective into a situation without causing offense. Saying, "I don't think you have any intent to learn the guitar...you never bring your instrument to the lesson," would certainly offend.

Another thing that I have done that works well is ask a friend, who is not involved in the situation, to act as a mediator. This friend can say directly what I cannot say, and will do so while I am somewhere else. "Matthew is upset with you because you took his bicycle without asking him first. It is important to him to know what's going on. He thought someone had stolen it and was about

---

لي ماعندوه قلم ولا دوية مامعول على القرية 1

to report it to the police." I may never actually talk about the situation with the person causing me the problem, but we will both know what the other is thinking this way. The third party will usually speak very directly and clearly on behalf of each of us and work hard to smooth things over.

Unity within a community is important in a place where people used to (and sometimes still) live their whole lives in the neighborhood where they were born. They think, "If this is someone I will have to see for the rest of my life, then I don't want there to be bad blood between us forever." In a situation like this, good relationships are more important than who is right. That would have rung truer in the days of nomadic tribes or inter-village warfare when the lives of people in the community were completely interdependent.

If things get to a point where I cannot communicate my thoughts effectively without being direct, then I will prepare the listener to hear the bad news. "Look, you are my friend. I love you like a brother. You know that you are important to me and that I respect you. Still, I think you're wrong." In this way I am telling the person that they are valuable to me and that I don't want what I have to say to come between us, but rather that I want to work it out. This is a less common solution here, and is therefore not as well-rehearsed. It ends up being far more difficult, but I have had it work.

66

There's always a twist

هدا طبيب ديال الحماق و بغى يعرف واش مرضة دياله صحة ولا
لا. داهم لي بيسين خوي و جلس باش يشوف شنو غادي يوقع.
واحد منهم شاف البيسين، جرى له، قفز و ظرب راسه علاحقاش
ماكاينش في الماء. شي اخر شاف البيسين و ستعمل الدروج باش
يدخل علاحقاش فكر بلي الماء بارد بزاف. كان واحد لي جلس في
الأرض و مادار والو. فكر الطبيب، "ممكن هو صح." مشا عنده و
طلب علاش مادار كيف خوته. جوب، "الى غرقت، واش غادي
تعتقني؟"

*There was a doctor for the insane and one day he wanted
to find out if his patients were healthy or not. He took
three of them to an empty swimming pool and sat down to
see what would happen. One man ran to the pool, jumped
in and hit his head because there was no water. The
second man tried to enter the pool slowly using the stairs
because he thought the water was cold. The last one sat
down and did nothing. The doctor wondered if he might*

be healthy so we went to him to ask why he hadn't done like his brothers[1]. The man responded, "If I drown, will you save me?"

This joke has so many variations I have lost count. In fact, I'm sure I remember fewer than half of the ones I have heard.

There's the one about the time the doctor took the patients to a room with no doors or windows (like when you watch a good Hollywood movie, suspension of disbelief is required here). He takes out a pen and draws a door on the wall and watches. One guy hurts his head trying to knock the door down. Another keeps trying unsuccessfully to grab the doorknob and open the door. The third sits down. When asked why he didn't do like his brothers I have heard two different replies, both of which amuse me. In one account he simply says, "I don't have the key." In another he looks serious and says, "Shh. I have

---

1 It is common in Moroccan culture to call people "brother" even when they are not a part of your family, or in this instance, part of the same family. The doctor uses "brothers" here to emphasize that all three men are together in the same situation.

the key in my pocket."

Another time the doctor takes them to an empty room and tells the patients there is a party. Some dance to the imaginary music. Others try to eat the non-existent food. One lady[1] sits and does nothing. When asked why she doesn't do like her brothers she replies, "I'm the bride."[2]

The key to each of these is the unexpected, but logical twist. Granted, the patients are still insane, but their explanations actually make some sense within their falsely constructed worlds.

If we look closely at ourselves and our home

---

1 This is the only time I've heard a version of this joke with a woman in it and it certainly wouldn't make any sense otherwise.

2 It might help if I note here that at Moroccan wedding parties the bride sits on a special platform wearing stunningly beautiful clothes and participates very little in the revelry, except as an observer. She will slip out occasionally to change into another equally beautiful outfit, only to return to her throne and preside over the festivities. The only other time I have seen the bride get up is when certain of her family/friends pick up her throne while she is sitting on it and dance/carry her around the party while singing and chanting. It's quite fun, really.

societies we will discover that almost every happening, action and tradition, from covering your mouth when you yawn, to extending a hand to shake as a greeting, has an explanation of some sort, if only we are willing to dig deep enough to discover it. Those we can't figure out we presume had a reason at some time, but the reason has been lost.

Humans tend to perceive the world in such a way that we are unconsciously unwilling to admit that things may happen or exist without an underlying cause or meaning. It seems that our emotional and psychological health depend, to some extent, on making sense out of our world. We can handle chaos and mystery for a time, but eventually we want to know; we want something solid to hold on to as an explanation.

Social psychologists have come up with a theory which says that people prefer an absurd reason over no reason. That is, we will grasp for any explanation available to try to understand our surroundings, even if we know the reason is illogical.

In my opinion these jokes are not only about "crazy" people; we laugh at them because they reveal to us a little bit about ourselves. We have a strong distaste for the mysterious and we will either do all in our power to uncover that which is hidden, or we will reach out for the nearest explanation we find that seems remotely possible. This is true in the West and it is also true in the East. It is true in older and newer societies. It is true in Morocco.

Morocco is a land where superstition runs deep. It is a land of mystery, a land of intrigue, a land where, up until recently, only a few people were privileged with good education. Even as the country strives to educate its population, the most recent figures I have seen report that only half of the people are functionally literate. This number is rising steadily, however, and the percentage is significantly higher among those under 30 years of age.

Like people all around the world, Moroccans want to understand what is happening around them. At times they may resign themselves to the mysterious and unknowable will of God, but if it is remotely possible, they want to know why things happen. Even the typical response, "It was God's will," hints at a grasping for the existence of underlying meaning in confusing events.

In a highly illiterate and community driven society

rumors can start and spread very quickly. The winter of 2005, there was a rumor that someone in Morocco had died of the Bird Flu that was engulfing the world with fear. Chicken prices dropped because people quit buying them. I was told the crisis ended when the king was seen eating chicken on television without getting sick[1]. People needed someone in authority, someone they trusted to prove to them the rumors were false. It wasn't enough that the supposed death had never been substantiated (and actually had not occurred). An appeal to a higher power or authority was needed.

Every place I have been in Morocco has a mosque, not just every city, but every neighborhood. Far less known is that nearly every neighborhood also has a sahher,[2] a magician or sorcerer. This is a witch doctor who will concoct potions, cast spells, write special prayers or talismans to put in your amulet of protection and a ton of other interesting things.

---

1 Even if this never happened, the rumor that the king had eaten chicken in public with no negative repercussions would be enough to dispel the rumors.

2 سحر

This person's goal (at least those that truly believe in what they are doing and who are not intentional charlatans) is to help a powerless individual regain some control through magic charms and occult practices. In most cases I have heard or know of, these are men. In some cases they are even the local Imam (Muslim leader within the community)[1] who leads the prayers and may teach at the mosque.

If that isn't enough to satisfy the curious or worried, it seems each neighborhood also has a local seer[2] or fortune teller. This is someone who will gladly attempt to tell you what has happened, is happening or will happen

---

1 I know that many Muslims reading this will immediately disagree and say these things are incompatible with "true" or "pure" Islam. Having studied the faith according to what the books tell us, I would tend to agree. However, in practice, what I am describing is the position that these people are given in many communities. This is how they are perceived and treated by the masses. In regard to religion, I am not intending to write about the theoretical or theological aspects, but rather what I have observed being practiced. I will leave the argument regarding who is and who is not a Muslim to others.

2 شوفة

for a small fee. They may be sorcerers as well, but not necessarily. Interestingly, these are often women.

This is a land that overwhelmingly believes in things beyond what can be seen with the eyes or observed using the scientific method. In some cases this comes as a direct result of a persistent and genuine faith in God and in the Qur'an, which speaks of angels, demons, life after death and beings called jinns[1]. In other cases, people's thoughts and feelings have been manipulated, using a belief in the supernatural, to get people to act a certain way.

Maybe that is where the common fear of pouring hot water down a sink drain came from. I have repeatedly been told that jinns live in drains and that they don't like hot water. Perhaps a plumber once made a poor repair on a drain using something that would be dissolved in hot water. Maybe he covered up his incompetence by using a story he heard about jinns liking holes in the ground,

---

1 These beings can be good or evil. They can be kind, helpful, mischievous, or evil. In any case, it is reputedly hard to tell the difference, so most people say the best thing to do is avoid them. This is also the root from which we get the English word "genie."

modifying it to keep an uneducated soul from undoing his faulty repair...it's just a theory, but that's what this chapter is all about; trying to make sense of my surroundings.

Society's foundation

هاذي واحد المدرسة فيها أستاذ جديد. بغى يعرف سميات ديال الطلاميد و بدأ يسولهم، "شكون أنت، شكون أنتي." جاوب الأول بلي سميته يوسف. طلب الأستد نوض و قول سورة ْ يوسف. جاوبات الاثانية بلي سميتها مريم. طلب الأستاذ نوضي و قولي سورة ْ مريم. شاف شي بنت حداها و هي خافت. جاوبات، "أنا، سميتي فاتحة."

There was a new teacher at the school and he wanted to know the names of all his students. He asked them, "Who are you?" and they began to answer. The first said, "I'm Yosef" and was then told to stand and recite Surat Yosef. The second said, "I'm Miryam" and was told to stand and recite Surat Miryam. Next to her was a frightened little girl who answered, "My name is Fatiha!"

It is impossible to understand Moroccan culture

without a basic understanding of Islam. At a minimum, one should know what the Qur'an is, what the five pillars of the Islamic faith are, and have some knowledge of the religion's basic beliefs. I will cover some of these in this chapter.

The Qur'an is the key to understanding this joke. The Qur'an is the holy book of Islam. It is said to be an eternal book existing in heaven that was revealed bit by bit over many years to an illiterate man named Mohamed, in a series of angelic visitations. The angel told Mohamed to memorize and recite several passages, called suras or surat. He did so and taught others to memorize the passages as well.

After Mohamed's death all of the suras were written down and collected in the form in which we now find them. They are mostly ordered according to length, from the longest to the shortest, with one exception being the sura called the "Fatiha" or the opening, the beginning. This first sura is among the shortest and is one which is recited every time a Muslim prays.

There are ladies named Fatiha throughout the Arabic speaking world. The name is not an uncommon one. What makes this joke funny is that it is probably not this particular girl's name. She saw her friends, Yosef and Miryam, have to recite extremely long suras simply because they had the same name as that sura. This girl, through quick thinking, saved herself a lot of work. I have heard another variation of this joke in which the girl answers with the name of the second sura, which is also short and is recited by Muslims during their prayers. That variation is either funnier or less so, depending on your sense of humor. The second sura is named Baqara, "The Cow."

The Islamic religion stands on five actions called "The Pillars." They are the testimony, prayer, giving alms, fasting, and the pilgrimage.[1] According to Muslim

---

1 The shahada or testimony is the statement of faith for all Muslims, "There is no God but God and Mohamed is his prophet." Salat or prayers are to be performed five times daily. Zakat, alms, are to be given to the poor with an annual minimum, which is a percentage of all assets. Sawm, or fasting, is required for all Muslims during the month of Ramadan and considered meritorious at other times. Finally, the hajj, the pilgrimage to Mecca, is required once in a lifetime of all who can afford to make it.

teaching, all a person has to do to be a Muslim is say the testimony and truly believe it, and then try to perform all of these pillars sincerely.

There are some basic beliefs in Islam, but contrary to a faith like Christianity, which stresses orthodoxy, or correct belief, Islam stresses orthopraxy, or correct action. This is an important difference because it allows for a wide variety of specific beliefs to exist under the blanket of Islam. What is important is the testimony and the striving to complete the pillars. Anything else is secondary. There are a very small number of beliefs that are required in Islam.

The first and most vital of Muslim beliefs is the unity of God. In Islam there is only one God, and he accepts no partners. God is one. This is called the tawhid, and along with an acceptance of Mohamed as the prophet of God, the tawhid forms the basis for all faith.

Some of the other foundational tenets of Islam include a belief that God has sent many prophets, but that Mohamed is the last and greatest among them. One must also believe in angels, in sacred books (all of which are usually said to have been lost or corrupted except for the

Qur'an), in a final judgment of all people before God's throne, at which time he will decide whether a person spends eternity in heaven or hell, and finally, God's absolute sovereignty.

This final doctrine, God's sovereignty, is important because it means that God is ruled by no one and by nothing outside of himself. It is impossible to know with any certainty what God will do. One must rely on God's will and favor, even regarding the final judgment. To say that one is assured of going to heaven is the equivalent of saying that God has limits and that his thoughts can be known by mere mortals...this is akin to heresy.

It has been my experience that it is impossible in Morocco to have a conversation on any topic with anyone without God entering the discussion. There is an alternating sense of security and resignation in a life that is lived in surrender to the idea that God has foreordained what will happen, and that nothing can be done to alter his will. This has a profound impact on societal actions, trends, beliefs and understandings, and must be a part of any serious attempt to understand Moroccan culture.

Your words don't matter

هدا مش مشى الحج. و رجع و الفران شاوه فيه. قال واحد، دابا هو
خونا بالدين. خصنا نرحبو به. مشى الفار ليه و القط حول يشده.
الفار رجع لي الاخورين و قال، في برى هو حاج ولكن القلب ديالو
مازال قط.

*There was a cat who went on the pilgrimage to Mecca.
When he returned, the mice saw him and one said, "The
cat is now our brother," and went to welcome him. When
he got close, the cat tried to catch him. The mouse
returned to his family and said, "On the outside he's a
Hajj[1] but in his heart he's still a cat.*

Religion, specifically Islam, plays a huge role in
Moroccan society at every level. From the palace of the
king, all the way down to the most humble home of the

---

1 A term of respect given to one who has performed the hajj.

poorest person in a rural village, Islam is hailed as the rule for daily life. It is the foundation for government, society, relationships, health and welfare, and a myriad of other things. This is what everyone says.

As in any society and religion, however, words and ideals do not always match actions. Even the best of intentions may fail. Additionally, one cannot ignore that there are people whose intentions are not as high and lofty as their words may appear. These are the ones this joke takes exception to.

This is not a joke against Islam nor any aspect of it. It is intended to highlight that one should not measure a man based on what they say or what they wear[1], but instead by their actions. The joke is not saying the pilgrimage is good or bad, but rather that going on the pilgrimage does not in and of itself make a person more respectable. Honor should be earned over time and with deeds of kindness, honesty and justice, not from the mere act of taking a trip...even a trip commanded by God.[2]

---

1 Often a Hajj will wear a different style of clothing or style their hair in a new way to set them apart from the community.

2 It is interesting to note that people who are respected in this

One may be obedient in deeds and not submissive in the heart. This joke says that this sort of obedience is of absolutely no value whatsoever.

Worldwide, there are a number of people who claim to follow their religion from their heart but whose actions consistently tell a different story. We're all human. This joke, however, isn't about the occasional slip up or bad day; it is about hypocrisy.

Once, I was sitting in a government office waiting for a courier to arrive, to see if a paper I needed had been completed and signed. I have done this many times, and I have been treated very well in government offices all over the country. Sometimes employees are tired or maybe a little overworked and get a little gruff, but that happens. This particular day was different.

The paper I was waiting for was necessary, so I needed and wanted to stay on the workers' good side. Their work was the key to my living in their country. One slip and I might have to leave. I was not interested in discussing anything controversial with them, nor did I

culture are often referred to as "Hajj," even if they have never made the pilgrimage. This helps to illustrate my point.

want to do anything other than have them like me while I was there and forget me once I left with the paper I needed.

As it happened, work was slow that day, so the workers took advantage of the rare opportunity to speak with, and solicit the opinions of an Arabic speaking American, a genuine rarity. They asked me my opinions on Afghanistan, Iraq, Palestine/Israel, George W. Bush, and a host of other political issues. Then they asked me if I had become a Muslim *yet*.

The manner of the question didn't thrill me. "Yet?" I have no intention of becoming a Muslim. I answered that I have nothing against people being free to believe in Islam, but that I have no desire to change my religion. Immediately, I was told that was fine and it is a horrible crime to try to change another person's religion, that one should never do so[1]. This was followed by another

---

1 I don't think it's bad to talk about what you believe or to want others to agree with you. I've found that people only accept responsibility for themselves, their behavior, and their faith if they choose it freely without any outside pressure or incentive. Using a position of power or influence to make people listen to

employee telling me that we should all respect one another's beliefs.

I told a story about how you can tell whether a person is good or bad. I said it isn't by what they wear or the words they say, it is by the results of their life. I pointed out the window at some trees and said, "How do you know that is an orange tree and that one is an olive tree?" Everyone answered, "By the fruit on the trees." I said, "The fruit of your life will tell the people around you what kind of person you are."

Then, the three workers present each told me in his own way that I seem to be a good person, so most certainly God will bring me into Islam. They then asked me several times whether I wanted to become a Muslim, if I had ever read the Qur'an[1], and implying with each question that I was less of a person because I am not a Muslim.

What alternately amuses and frustrates me here is

---

you talk about your religion as a form of religious or political proselytizing is as abhorrent to me as is the giving of jobs, "sparing of lives" or other incentives in exchange for conversion.

1 I have read the Qur'an. In fact, I have even read it in Arabic.

that I have had this conversation at least a hundred times in different places. These are generally good people who mean well, but many don't believe what they are telling me —that everyone should be allowed to follow whatever religion he wants to follow without being pressured or even encouraged to change it.

The law in Morocco forbids proselytizing in any form so I'm not surprised that people say it is a bad thing to do. The law hasn't changed people's hearts, though, so they are living what they believe...that I should become a Muslim. At least on the surface.

Far more interesting and amusing to me are the numerous times I have had this conversation with someone that I know doesn't live according the the most basic of Islamic tenets. I've actually confronted a couple of people on this[1] and been told, "Islam commands that I try to convince you to become a Muslim," as the person shrugs off responsibility for their actions[2].

---

1 Not, however, while waiting in their office for a paper I need them to sign.

2 One of the more amusing times this happened was when the offer to convert to Islam was followed by an attempt to give me some

My point is that the people around you know you by your actions, no matter how well you think you have hidden the more unholy ones. Nobody is fooled forever by pretentious exteriors and zealous words, and there are many who see through them immediately.

That is the point of this joke. You can wear the right clothes, you can say the right words, you can pray perfectly and have the answers to every question that may come up, but if your heart is hard, the world will ultimately know you for who and what you are.

I've chosen not to include any of the dozens of jokes I have been told about unholy Imams, some who are greedy, some who are proud, some who are lustful.[1] Any one of them could serve to continue the discussion of this topic. I left them out because it is not my goal to offend anyone and I respect the people who genuinely believe and try to follow their beliefs.

I included this joke about the cat who went on the hajj to highlight the power of community to lead, direct, and even control the actions and words of followers. The

---

hashish resin to snort. I politely refused both offers.

1   All of which could be equally applied to an unholy priest or rabbi.

community is more important here than the individual, and the respect of the community is more important than the truth.

Acceptance by others is vital to life, not just here in Morocco, but everywhere. We all need friends, family, and a place to belong. We are all willing, at times, to compromise ourselves in one way or another in our attempt to do that.

Some people will compromise their personal wants and desires to try to conform to community standards in a feeble attempt to hold on to position or respect. Others will sacrifice their public image for the sake of belonging to a community that, while at times small or hidden, more accurately reflects their beliefs and standards. In either case, a person's true self will eventually be seen and known through his actions.

I'll do here what I did there

واحد نهار جحا كان مصافر و وصل قرية جديدة. خل الحمار
ديال في الزنقة و دخل الحانوت. ملي رجع الحمار ماكاينش.
وقف جحا في وسط الزنقة و غوت، "إلى ماعطيتونيش حماري
ندير لي ديرت فالمدينة الأخرة." و دخل مقهى. بعد شي سعة رجع
و كان حمار دياله. ركب عليه و مشى. الناس في القرية كانو
كيخمّمو اش دار فالمدينة الأخرة و صايفتو ولد يطلب منه أش
دار تمة. جاوب جحا، "أنا مشيت."

*One day while traveling, Juha arrived at a village he had
never been to before. He left his donkey in the street and
went into a shop. When he came back his donkey was
missing. Juha stood in the middle of the street and yelled,
"If my donkey isn't here when I get back I'll do here what
I did in the other village!" Then he entered a cafe. An
hour later he returned and his donkey was there. He got
on and rode out of town. The townspeople were
wondering what Juha had done in the other town so they*

sent a boy to ask him. Juha replied, "I left."

Fear of the unknown is a powerful force. It can paralyze and it can motivate. Juha uses that to his advantage here. Someone has stolen his donkey, he doesn't know who and he really has no recourse. It isn't likely that the members of a small village would turn over one of their own, even if they all want him to be punished. Admitting to an outsider that there is a thief among them would bring shame on the entire village. What can Juha do?

Notice that he doesn't threaten anyone directly. He doesn't ask them to turn over the thief to be brought to justice. He doesn't initiate a direct confrontation with the entire community that he would be sure to lose. Instead, he appeals to their fear of the unknown.

"I'll do here what I did in the other village!" Which village? Where? No one knows. Juha has never been to this village, no one knows him. He could be a powerful magician, a sorcerer. He might put a curse on the village, its crops, its flocks, its people. He might be a great friend of the jinns, like Sulayman is said to have been. Maybe

Juha would call on their assistance to come and punish the townspeople. There's no way of knowing what he is capable of and the villagers decide they can't take the risk.

Because Juha gave them a way to make restoration without losing face, it was easy for them to recover his donkey and get it back in its place before Juha returned. When Juha saw his donkey, he most likely decided this village was not a place where he really wanted to be, so he leaves.

The townspeople were left wondering what sort of power Juha might have. What could he have done if they had had not appeased him? Nothing, it turned out.

There are many layers to this story. The first is superstition, which is most prevalent among the uneducated. As discussed in a previous chapter, when things are not understood through education or direct experience, humans attempt to comprehend their environment using the most reasonable explanation available.

There is also a subtle and minor religious element to this story. Remember, you cannot divorce Islam from Moroccan culture, as it has had a great impact on every area of thought and action. Islam teaches the reality of the supernatural realm and the existence of angels, devils and jinn. While the most conservative forms of Islamic thought and teaching may forbid and even deny the power of sorcery, the more popular folk beliefs confirm and in some cases even encourage it.

Juha is neither a saint nor a villain. Typically, he fills the role of the fool in the king's court. As I mentioned before, he is someone who speaks the truth when others cannot, for better and for worse. Sometimes what he reveals is beautiful and desirable, and other times it is painful and difficult.

Traditionally, a traveler in Morocco is treated with great respect and kindness. Upon arriving in a new town, I have often been invited to people's homes, treated to a wonderful hot meal, and even invited to stay the night in their spare bedroom. There is a proverb here that says a person should be willing to starve so that their guest may feast. I have seen this proverb lived out several times.

In this instance, the subtext of what Juha is saying is that he realizes he has no real power to make a community which he is not a part of conform to its stated values (i.e.

stealing is wrong, the traveler should be given hospitality). What can he do? If he tries to confront them he will likely end up in a worse condition than he already is. Instead, he reveals to them their sin and their slavery to the fear of the unknown.

"If my donkey is not returned..." says, "There is a thief among you. I don't know who he is and I don't care. I want my donkey back." Following it with, "I'll do here what I did in the other village," immediately strikes fear in the hearts of the people.

It is the last line of the joke, however, that is the most telling. Juha could have said anything in response to the question of what he did. He could have made up a grandiose story of magic and power. He could have simply refused to answer and kept the village in fear in case he wanted to return someday. He did neither.

Juha intentionally sacrificed his position of power over the village and told them the truth. What makes the joke both funny and painful is that the truth produces more shame for the villagers than any of the other options. The villagers believed he was greater than them. They feared he might have supernatural powers. Juha never directly claimed any of these things for himself. The villagers deceived themselves.

As a result of their ignorance and superstition, the village had bound itself to a fear of sorcerous punishment. This fear was appropriate in one sense because the villagers all knew that someone among them had acted dishonorably. As a result, the community deserved to be punished. This fed into the religious foundation of their community and the knowledge that those who do such things deserve to burn in hell. The terror increased.

I find it interesting that Juha never lets the villagers off the hook. He merely points out their fallen condition and leaves them to figure out what to do next. I'm not sure what else to say about that or what meaning this may have, but it is an interesting phenomenon. Perhaps the story was originally intended as a morality tale or perhaps as a discussion starter. It could also be that the original author simply thought it was enough to show the bad people receiving their due and chose to leave the resolution to the imagination of the listener.

Who should I believe in?

قال لك هذي مرأ من العربية مشات لطبيب. قال ليها الطبيب تحيد الحوايج ديالها باش يقلبها. فجوبات لا حشومة، أنا مزوجة. رجعات و سولات راجلها. قال هاذا عادي عند الدوكتور. مشات عود ثاني لالطبيب، طلبها تحيد خوايجها. جوبات، "واخة، أنت فلول."

There once was a young country girl who went to the doctor. The doctor asked her to take off her clothes so he could examine her. She replied that this was shameful and besides, she was married. She went home and asked her husband about it and he told her it is normal to do this at the doctor's office. She returned to the doctor, who again asked her to remove her clothes. She replied, "Okay, but you first."

Who are you most likely to believe? Who do you trust when you hear advice or information? This is an interesting question in any society. Some will probably say, "I trust the experts, the scientists, the researchers, the leaders." Others may answer, "I trust my friends and their advice above all." A Moroccan would likely answer, "My family."

On the surface, this is just a silly joke about a naive country girl and her misunderstanding of what goes on in a doctor's office. Some might take it for another example of the tension between rural and urban cultures. Others may say it demonstrates yet again the arrogance of the educated over the trust of the simple. I think it is a great opportunity to discuss which sources of information are deemed reliable and why.

A common proverb in Morocco says, "Don't ask the doctor, ask the one who has had the disease."[1] There is an innate mistrust of outsiders in this society. Relationships tend to gain trust according to how long they have existed, and the familial proximity of the individual in question. Degrees are nice, education is good, but personal knowledge of the individual is far more valuable when

---

1 سول المجارب و ما تسول الطبيب

attempting to establish trust.

When I was a child, there was a well known television commercial in the United States that stated something like, "Seven out of ten doctors recommend sugarless gum for their patients who chew gum." For most people in Morocco that information would be meaningless. It wouldn't help them decide whether to chew that gum or not. However, if seven out of ten people in their neighborhood chewed that brand of gum, they would be extremely likely to try it. If seven out of ten people in their immediate family chewed that brand of gum, the seven who chewed it would wonder what was wrong with the other three.

Sometimes, this phenomenon manifests itself as similar to peer pressure, but I see it as something deeper and less sinister. We must remember that both traditional Arab and Berber societies have their foundations among nomadic desert tribes. Trust of one another within the tribe was vital for survival. Outsiders might want to take your food, your flocks, or your women. Trust was not easily given to outsiders, who might be trying to deceive for personal gain, especially if what they said contradicted what was known, or presumed true, among tribal members.

Even now that most Moroccans live in large cities, some of that ethos has survived. If an outsider presents a new product or process, or makes claims about an existing one, most Moroccans will begin the consideration of the product, process or claim by asking their family and friends for their opinions. Often, this will follow an initial rejection of whatever has been presented. The process might look something like this:

Rachid: "Sugarless gum? Who ever heard of such a silly thing. Get that stuff away from me."

Latif: "The dentist says it is better for your teeth. Too much sugar is bad for you."

Rachid: "Who cares what the dentist says? Sugarless gum? That's crazy."

...minutes later...

Rachid: "Hey, Hamid! I met this guy selling gum that doesn't have sugar in it. Have you ever heard that?"

Hamid: "Yeah. My cousin started chewing it and he hasn't had any new problems with his teeth."

Rachid: "Hmm. Maybe I'll give it a try."

What makes Rachid more willing to try the gum? He has heard of the experience of his friend's cousin...it's all about relationship. Someone he knew was able to speak from secondhand experience, based on the firsthand experience of someone he knew well (even if Rachid heard about it thirdhand).

What made the young country girl willing to abandon her social more against disrobing in front of a man? The word of her husband that this is normal in a doctor's office. She didn't even understand why she was taking her clothes off, but her husband said it was normal and she trusted him.

This is a society where new ideas are slow to penetrate and even slower to be accepted. One must be patient when introducing something no one has experienced locally. It will help if it is something that Moroccans who have lived overseas have used or experienced, as long as those Moroccans have retained ties and relationships within their homeland. Some good examples are Pepsi Cola or maybe the new "Mecca Cola" that was introduced in 2004 or 2005, which claimed to give a portion of all profits to Islamic charities. Neither of these has sold well, even though they are cheaper than Coca Cola. Why? Because everyone knows Coca Cola. Everyone has tried Coke. Their friends and families are familiar with it. Why switch to something else that is unknown and unfamiliar, especially if it is just about the same?

Some Muslims have warned of Christians coming into Morocco in an attempt to convert Muslims to Christianity. At times they have been quite vocal in their opposition to the very idea and cried out for public action against such things. It is already illegal to attempt to persuade someone to change their religion. I'm convinced most attempts to do so are unlikely to be fruitful here and that there is very little for this vocal minority to worry about. Why?

First, people accept responsibility for their behaviors and beliefs only if they have chosen them without outside pressures and influences. This means that those Moroccans who have freely chosen to follow Islam as their faith and the faith of their ancestors and country are not going to be easily swayed to follow anything else.

Those who might feel or experience any outside

pressure or influence from a foreigner to convert are not likely to make a true conversion in their heart. Some may exhibit an outward conversion in the hope of receiving monetary reward or to obtain a job from a foreigner, but this doesn't seem likely to happen in my opinion and I would imagine it would be short lived if it did happen.

Second, this is a society where the opinion of the community and the family bear more weight and authority than the opinion of an outsider. A Moroccan would have to be completely disillusioned with or disconnected from his family, friends and their faith to willingly leave it. Unless entire families or neighborhoods were to choose to convert together (through some sort of divine assistance), I wouldn't expect more than the occasional societal outsider to make a change of this nature any more than he would choose to paint his face blue and dance the tango in the street.

I have heard some interesting ideas during my years in Morocco. Some have told me that I need to keep the windows closed at all times while traveling in a motorized vehicle, because the draft from an open window will make me sick. I was told this in the heat of August. The same person absolutely forbid the air conditioner to be used because it also produced a sickness-inducing draft.

We could have a long discussion on the facts and falsehoods surrounding pregnancy. Eat this, avoid that, and if you do the following, you will have a boy. The list of old wives' tales is long. Some will shyly admit they don't actually believe any of them. However, grandma is the one who said it, and even if the instructions are wrong young people will often follow them so that they don't shame her or damage the relationship.

Regardless of what the belief is, once it has permeated Moroccan society it is difficult to change. That can be a good thing or a bad thing, depending on the belief, but it is not something that is likely to change. I consider Morocco to be like a large ship. It takes a long time and gentle adjustments to the rudder to turn. If you change things too quickly the ship will tip over and sink.

Epilogue

I have spent the last few weeks thinking about all that I have written in the previous chapters and I have begun the revision process. While doing so I happened to sit down with a Moroccan acquaintance who asked me how this book was progressing. During our conversation he asked me what sorts of things I had seen that I liked about Moroccan culture and what things bothered me.

In the chapter, "Respect is more important than truth," I wrote about an incident where a policeman stopped me and asked me for a bribe. I relayed this story to my acquaintance, who had a completely different understanding of the matter. It is his perspective that I would like to share as a fitting end to this text.

Before I do so, let me tell you a little bit about the man. He is relatively wealthy and owns several businesses.

He speaks multiple languages and when he was younger he had the opportunity to live in Europe for a time. He has also traveled to the United States. This is a person whom I would classify as upper middle class.

I described to him the first half of my story, that I had been stopped, that my papers had been examined and returned to me. I mentioned that the policeman had told me what the fine would be according to the law, if he decided to write a citation. I relayed how the officer asked me if I wanted a ticket, and after my negative response, proceeded to ask me what I would give him instead.

At this point the man interrupted me, so I never finished the story. I was so intrigued by what he was saying that I spent the next half an hour asking him multiple follow up questions. I wanted to be certain I understood him correctly.

"Wait! You can't be upset about that. The officer was being kind to you," he interrupted. "He could have charged you 400 Dirhams and instead was being merciful by giving you the option to pay less, as a reminder to obey the law, without you being forced to bear its fullest punishment."

Intrigued I responded, "So it was okay that he asked me for a bribe? That's illegal, isn't it?"

"The law exists as a set of **guidelines** so we know what is right and what is wrong. No one is perfect, we can't be expected to do everything correctly all of the time. This man was being kind to you by not making you pay the full penalty because he realizes that we are all imperfect."

"But isn't bribery wrong?" I prodded.

"Look, he asked you to pay him. He will have to pay half of that money to his boss who will then have to pay half of all that he receives to his boss and so on, all the way to the top. You can't change the system. It is what it is."

I was taken aback. I have no idea whether this accusation is true or false, but the person making it was absolutely convinced. I decided I needed to press further.

I continued, "I don't know whether that is true or false and I'm not sure I want to know. I haven't had this experience before. I am curious, though, do you think bribery is right or wrong?"

Indignantly he replied, "It happens all over the world. Do you think police and government officials in America don't ask for and accept bribes? Europe? Are you saying your country is better than mine?"

"That has nothing to do with my question. Whether this happens other places or not I want to know what *you* think. Is bribery a sin?" I asked, deliberately changing the word I used in the question to push the point further. My answer came by way of a story.

"Suppose the policeman stopped a hardworking handyman, someone who was honest and did his job well but didn't have a lot of money. Let's say the man was riding his motor[1] down the street and he ran a red light. The policeman would have to stop him if he saw it happen because it is his job to keep people safe.

"He would instruct the man to always stop when the light is red, otherwise he could get hit by a car and injured or even die. The policeman would know that the laborer wasn't a rich man and couldn't actually afford to pay a 400

---

1 A moped or vélomoteur, it's like a bicycle with a motor or a small, underpowered motorcycle with pedals you crank to start the motor.

Dirham fine, but to make sure the man remembers in the future, the policeman would penalize him in some way. So he would ask him for an amount of money adequate to make the handyman think before breaking the law again in the future. For some, that might be only 20 Dirhams, for others 100 Dirhams. The amount of the fine would vary according to the ability of the person to pay. They might even bargain a bit."

"Are you serious?" I interjected with fascination.

"Yes," my acquaintance continued. "Look at the income tax in your country. Does everyone pay the same amount? Does everyone pay even the same percentage? There are even some who don't have to pay taxes at all. Why? It's mercy. Those who have more pay a little extra to help cover for those who don't have as much."

I began to say, "But the income tax is not illegal. Bribery is." However, my friend's cell phone rang and he had to leave. The conversation ended there. We smiled at each other, shook hands, kissed cheeks and went our separate ways, he to a meeting and me to my office filled with wonder and doubt as to whether anything I have understood or written thus far is accurate.

I am choosing to end this book with a realization. I began the book stating that I am not an expert on Moroccan culture, but merely a continuing student. I end it now with the revelation that the more I learn, the more I realize I have left before me to explore. I most certainly remain a student.

Final notes and thoughts

You may have noticed the license under which I have released this work. Let me take a moment and explain why I have done this, rather than reserve all of the rights for myself. This work is definitely copyrighted, you can see that on one of the first pages. I am the copyright holder. I have created this work for several purposes, one of which is that I hope to make some money from it. However, this is not the only reason for publishing this book. My greatest hope is that other people will find the information contained within it useful. I have given you, the reader, permission to copy, distribute, display and perform this work, and to make derivative works, as long as you follow a few simple rules on which I will now comment.

First, you have to make sure and tell everyone that I

am the author and owner of the copyright. In other words, you can copy it for your personal use or even for others to benefit from, but you can't claim that you are the author.

Second, you may not use this work for commercial purposes—that's my prerogative and my privilege alone as the creator of the work. I'm happy for you to use it as you like and even share it, but any money made from this work should be made by me.

Finally, if you alter, transform or build upon this work for any purpose other than personal use (that is, if you distribute your changes or additions) you must also release your work under this same license. You can be paid for your work, your additions or changes, but you have to let others use them in the same way I have let you use this work. Why?

It is my goal that as many people as possible benefit from this work. If you want to study it in a group and one person from the group buys a copy and then makes photocopies for the others in the group, I'm okay with that. If you can afford to, I would prefer that you each buy copies, but I'm not going to be persnickety about it as long as you don't sell the copies. I really hope that you will be able to make good use of the content that is in this work, that you feel free to discuss it, and learn from it.

I want you to feel free to make a study guide if you wish or recordings of the texts, a lexicon of the words or whatever else you might think up. However, if you do so, then I simply require that you treat me and others as I have treated you. I require that you release your work with the same availability and limits I have placed on this one so that others will benefit from your work just as you have benefited from mine. I also ask that you properly cite your original source (me). Sound fair? I think so. "Freely you received, so freely give."

Following in the same vein as the work's license, all the software and even the fonts used in creating this book are freely licensed and can be used and distributed without cost.

Selected Bibliography

These are but a small portion of the hundreds of books I have read in my continuing attempt to understand and improve my writing ability and my comprehension of Islamic, and more specifically, Moroccan culture.[1]

There are times when I feel I have understood and absorbed the material well, and other times when I have merely comprehended enough to spark further study. There are also times I have completely ignored or failed to heed the advice and instruction given in some of these texts, especially in the writing and style guides. I freely confess this is my fault and not that of the authors or publishers of those tomes. I hope you find this list useful.

---

1 As an aside, I'm still looking for a good collection of Moroccan jokes. Maybe that needs to be my next project.

History, religion and culture

Abdul Rauf, Imam Feisal. *What's Right With Islam: A New Vision for Muslims and the West.* New York: Harper-Collins. 2004.

Abouzaid, Leila and Barbara Parmenter, trans. and Elizabeth Fernea, introduction. *The year of the Elephant: A Moroccan Woman's Journey Toward Independence and other stories.* Austin, Texas: the Center for Middle Eastern Studies at The University of Texas at Austin. 1989.

Abouzaid, Leila and Heather Logan Taylor, trans. *Return to Childhood: The Memoir of a Modern Moroccan Woman.* Austin, Texas: University of Texas Press. 1998.

Abu-Lughod, Janet L. *Rabat: Urban Apartheid in Morocco.* Princeton, New Jersey: Princeton University Press. 1980.

Afkhami, Mahnaz, ed. *Faith and Freedom: Women's Human Rights in the Muslim World.* New York: Syracuse University Press. 1995.

Ali, Abdullah Yusuf. *The Meaning of the Holy Qur'an.* 9th ed, "new edition with revised translation, commentary and newly complied comprehensive index" in Arabic and English. Beltsville, Maryland: Amana Publications

Ali, Maulana Muhammad. *History of the Prophets: as narrated by the Holy Qur'an compared with the Bible.* Lahore: The Ahmadiyya Anjuman Ishaat Islam. 1996.

———. *Living Thoughts of the Prophet Muhammad.* Lahore: The Ahmadiyya Anjuman Ishaat Islam. 1992.

———. *Manual of Hadith, A.* Lahore: The Ahmadiyya Anjuman Ishaat Islam. date unknown.

Al-mamum Al-suhrawardy, Allama Sir Abdullah. *The Sayings of Muhammad.* forward by Mahatma Gandhi. Secaucus, New Jersey: Citadel Press. 1999.

Bowen, Donna Lee and Evelyn A. Early, editors. *Everyday Live in the Muslim*

Middle East. Bloomington and Indianapolis: Indiana University Press. 1993.

Bowles, Paul. *Collected Stories*. Santa Rosa: Black Sparrow Press. 1999.

————. *The Sheltering Sky*. New Jersey: The Ecco Press. 1949.

Brooks, Geraldine. *Nine Parts of Desire: The Hidden World of Islamic Women*. New York: Doubleday. 1995.

Burkhardt, Titus. *Fez: City of Islam*. Cambridge, UK: The Islamic Texts Society. 1992.

Burton, Sir Richard F. *A Personal Narrative of a Pilgrimage to Al-Madinah & Meccah*, vols. 1 and 2. New York: Dover Publications, Inc. 1964. (orig. ed. 1893)

Carroll, Raymonde. *Cultural Misunderstandings: The French-American Experience*. Trans. by Carol Volk. Chicago: The University of Chicago Press. 1988.

Chebel, Malek. *Symbols of Islam*. New York: Assouline Publishing. 2000.

Cornell, Vincent J. *Realm of the Saint: Power and Authority in Moroccan Sufism*. Austin, Texas: The University of Texas Press. 1998.

Dann, Robert. *Pretty as a Moonlit Donkey: a whimsical jaunt down the proverbial byways of Moroccan folklore*. Chester, England: Jacaranda Books. 2001.

Devine, Elizabeth and Nancy L. Braganti. *The Traveler's Guide to Middle Eastern and North African Customs & Manners*. New York: St. Martin's Press. 1991.

Dunn, Ross E. *The Adventures of Ibn Battuta: A Muslim Traveler of the 14ᵗʰ Century*. Berkeley and Los Angeles, California: University of California Press. 1986.

Dwyer, Kevin. *Moroccan Dialogues: Anthropology in Question*. Prospect Heights, IL: Waveland Press, Inc. 1987.

Esposito, John L. *Islam: The Straight Path*. Expanded ed. Oxford: Oxford University Press. 1991.

Fernea, Elizabeth Warnock. *A Street in Marrakech*. Prospect Heights, Illinois: Waveland Press, Inc. 1988.

Frishman, Martin and Hasan-Uddin Khan, editors. *The Mosque*. London: Thames & Hudson Ltd. 1994.

Gellner, Ernest and Charles Micaud. *Arabs & Berbers: From Tribe to Nation in North Africa*. Lexington, Massachusetts: Lexington Books. 1972.

Gettleman, Marvin E. and Stuart Schaar, editors. *The Middle East and Islamic World Reader*. New York: Grove Press. 2003.

Ghafoori, Ayatullah Dr. Ali. *The Ritual Prayer of Islam*. translated from Persian by Laleh Bakhtiar and Mohammad Nematzadeh. Houston, Texas: Free Islamic Literatures, Inc. 1982.

Harris, Walter. *Morocco That Was*. London: Eland Books and New York: Hippocrene Books, Inc. 1983. Originally published 1921.

Hillenbrand, Robert. *Islamic Art and Archetecture*. London: Thames and Hudson Ltd. 1999.

Hodges, Tony. *Western Sahara: The Roots of a Desert War*. Westport, Connecticut: Lawrence Hill & Co. 1983.

Hourani, Albert. *A History of the Arab Peoples*. Cambridge, Massachusetts: The Belknap Press of Harvard University Press. 1991.

Howe, Marvine. *Morocco: The Islamist Awakening and Other Challenges*. New York: Oxford University Press. 2005.

Huband, Mark. *Warriors of the Prophet: The Struggle for Islam*. Boulder, Colorado: Westview Press. 1999.

Hughes, Stephen O. *Morocco Under King Hassan*. Reading, UK: Ithaca Press. 2001.

Huntington, Samuel P. *The Clash of Civilizations and the Remaking of World Order*. New York: Simon & Schuster. 1996.

Ibn Khaldun. *The Muqaddimah: An Introduction to History*. Trans. by Franz Rosenthal. Abridged and edited by N. J. Daywood. Princeton, New Jersey: Princeton University Press. 2005.

Irwin, Robert, ed.. *Night & Horses & the Desert: An Anthology of Classical Arabic Literature*. Woodstock, New York: The Overlook Press, Peter Mayer Publishers Inc. 1999.

Kaandhlawi, Shaikhul Hadith Maulana Muhammad Zakariyya. *Stories of the*

Sahaabah: Teachings of Islam. trans. by Abdul Rashid Arshad. Chicago, Illinois: Kazi Publications Inc. no date.

King, Dean. *Skeletons on the Zahara: A True Story of Survival.* New York: Back Bay Books / Little, Brown and Company. 2004.

Lalami, Laila. *Hope and Other Dangerous Pursuits.* Chapel Hill, North Carolina: Algonquin Books of Chapel Hill. 2005.

Le Tourneau, Roger. *Fez in the Age of the Marinides.* Translated by Besse Alberta Clement. Norman, Oklahoma: University of Oklahoma Press. 1961.

Lewis, Bernard. *Muslim Discovery of Europe.* with a new introduction. New York: W. W. Norton and Company Ltd. 2001.

———. *What Went Wrong?: Western Impact and Middle Eastern Response.* Oxford: Oxford University Press. 2002.

Maalouf, Amin. *The Crusades Through Arab Eyes.* New York: Schocken Books. 1984.

Martin, Richard C. *Islamic Studies: A History of Religions Approach.* 2nd Ed. Upper Saddle River, New Jersey: Prentice Hall. 1996.

Maxwell, Gavin. *Lords of the Atlas: The Rise and Fall of the House of Glaoua 1893-1956.* New York: E. P. Dutton & Co., Inc. 1966.

Mernissi, Fatima. *Dreams of Trespass: Tales of a Harem Childhood.* Reading, Massachusetts: Addison-Wesley Publishing Company. 1994.

———. *Scheherazade Goes West: Different Cultures, Different Harems.* New York: Washington Square Press. 2001.

Messaoudi, Leila. *Proverbes et Dictons du Maroc.* (French/Arabic) Casablanca, Maroc: Belvisi. 1999.

Moon, Ross A. *About Islam.* Salt Lake City, Utah: Northwest Publishing, Inc. 1992.

Moroccan Literature in English: A Selection from the First Forum for Moroccan Creative Writers in English. Oujda, Maroc: Université Mohammed Premier Faculté des Lettres. 2001

Mostyn, Trevor and Albert Hourani, editors. *The Cambridge Encyclopedia of the Middle East.* Cambridge: Cambridge University Press. 1988.

Muhawi, Ibrahim and Sharif Kanaana. *Speak Bird, Speak Again: Palestinian Arab*

Folktales. Berkeley, California: University of California Press. 1989.

Naipul, V. S. *Beyond Belief: Islamic Excursions Among the Converted Peoples.* New York: Random House. 1998.

Nydell, Margaret K. *Understanding Arabs: A Guide for Westerners.* Yarmouth, Maine: Intercultural Press. 1987.

Oufkir, Malika and Michèle Fitoussi and Ros Schwartz, trans. *Stolen Lives: Twenty Years in a Desert Jail.* New York: Hiperion. 1999.

Pennell, C. R. *Morocco Since 1830: A History.* Washington Square, New York: New York University Press. 2000.

Peters, F. E. *The Hajj: the Muslim Pilgrimage to Mecca and the Holy Places.* Princeton, New Jersey: Princeton University Press. 1994.

Porch, Douglas. *The Conquest of Morocco.* New York: Farrar, Strauss and Giroux. 2005.

Rahman, Afzalur. *Muhammad: Encyclopedia of Seerah.* London: Seerah Foundation. 1981.

Robinson, Francis. *Cultural Atlas of the World, The: Islamic World since 1500.* Oxford: Stonehenge Press. 1992.

Schimmel, Annemarie. *Islamic Names.* Edinburgh: Edinburgh University Press. 1995.

Schulze, Reinhard. *A Modern History of the Islamic World.* Washington Square, New York: New York University Press. 2002.

Serwer-Bernstein, Blanche L. *In the Tradition of Moses and Mohammed: Jewish and Arab Folktales.* Northvale, New Jersey: Jason Aronson Inc. 1994.

Shaaban, Bouthania. *Both Right and Left Handed: Arab Women Talk About Their Lives.* Bloomington and Indianapolis: Indiana University Press. 1991.

Shah, Idries. *Tales of the Dervishes: Teaching Stories of the Sufi Masters over the Past Thousand Years.* New York: Arkana. 1993.

Spray, Lisa. *Women's Rights, the Quran and Islam.* Tucson, Arizona: BSM Press. 2002.

Viorst, Milton. *In the Shadow of the Prophet: The Struggle for the Soul of Islam.*

New York: Westview Press. 2001.

Warraq, Ibn. *Why I Am Not a Muslim.* New York: Prometheus Books. 1995.

Watt, Montgomery. *Muhammad: Prophet and Statesman.* Oxford: Oxford University Press. 1961.

Williams, John Alden. *Word of Islam, The.* Austin, Texas: University of Texas Press. 1994.

Arabic

المديني، احمد. <u>فاس...لو عادت إليه</u>. فاس: جميع الحقوق محفوظة للمؤلف.
2003

<u>مجمع الامثال</u>. بيروت، لبنان: دار الكتب العلمي. 1987

Language study aids

Abboud, Peter F. and Ernest N. McCarus, editors. *Elementary Modern Standard Arabic, volumes 1 & 2.* Cambridge: Cambridge University Press. 1968.

Agar, Michael. *Language Shock: Understanding the Culture of Conversation.* New York: Perennial / Harper Collins. 1994.

Bacon, Dan and Bichr Andjar and Abdennabi Benchehda. *Moroccan Arabic Phrasebook.* 2nd Ed. Hawthorn, Australia: Lonely Planet Publications. 1999.

Ennaji, Moha and Ahmed Makhoukh and Hassan Es-saiydy and Mohamed Moubtassime and Souad Slaoui. *Grammar of Moroccan Arabic, A.* Fès, Maroc: Université Sidi Mohamed Ben Abdellah Faculté des Lettres Dhar el Mehraz, Fès. 2004.

Harrell, Richard S. *A Basic Course in Moroccan Arabic.* Washington D. C.: Georgetown University Press. 1962.

————. *A Short Reference Grammar of Moroccan Arabic.* Washington D. C.:
Georgetown University Press. 1962.

Harrell, Richard S. and Harvey Sobelman. *A Dictionary of Moroccan Arabic:
English-Moroccan, Moroccan-English.* Washington D. C.: Georgetown
University Press. 1966.

Jenssen, Herbjørn. *The Subtleties and Secrets of the Arabic Language.* London:
Centre for Middle Eastern and Islamic Studies. 1998.

Khoury, Sadallah S. *The Correct Translator: For all Occasions Without a
Teacher. Arabic-English, English-Arabic.* A New Revised Edition. Beiruit: Al
Hayat Library. no date.

Nydell, Margaret K. *From Modern Standard Arabic to the Maghrebi Dialects
(Moroccan and Algerian): Conversion Course.* Arlington, VA: DLS Press. 1993.

Peace Corps – Morocco. *Moroccan Arabic, A Competency Based Curriculum.*
Rabat, Morocco. 1994.

Schultz, Eckehard and Gunther Krahl and Wolfgang Reuschel. *Standard Arabic: An
elementary-intermediate course.* Cambridge: Cambridge University Press. 2000.

Scott, G. C. *Practical Arabic...a comprehensive book for foreign learners.* Beiruit:
Librairie du Liban. 1978.

Writing

Axelrod, Rise B. and Charles C. Cooper. *The St. Martin's Guide to Writing.* 2nd Ed.
New York, St. Martin's Press, Inc. 1988.

The Chicago Manual of Style, 14th Ed. Chicago: The University of Chicago Press,
1993.

Gillespie, Sheena and Robert Singleton. *Across Cultures: A Reader for Writers.* 3rd
Ed. Needham Heights, Massachusetts: Allyn & Bacon. 1996.

King, Stephen. *On Writing: A Memoir of the Craft.* New York: Scribner. 2000.

Strunk, William Jr. and E. B. White. *The Elements of Style.* 4th Ed. Needham
Heights, Massachusetts: Allyn & Bacon, 2000.

Fonts used.

FreeSans and FreeSerif, Copyleft 2002, 2003, 2005 Free Software Foundation, www.gnu.org and www.fsf.org and directory.fsf.org/freefont.html for more information.

AlMohanad, Typeface and data © 2003, Arabeyes.org. This font is distributed under the terms of GNU General Public License, see www.gnu.org and www.fsf.org for more information.

CPSIA information can be obtained at www.ICGtesting.com
Printed in the USA
LVOW060827170812

294666LV00002B/4/P